Daydreams from the Ashes

K. Olsen

Published by K. Olsen, 2023.

While every precaution has been taken in the preparation of this book, the publisher assumes no responsibility for errors or omissions, or for damages resulting from the use of the information contained herein.

DAYDREAMS FROM THE ASHES

First edition. February 5, 2023.

Copyright © 2023 K. Olsen.

ISBN: 979-8215438053

Written by K. Olsen.

Table of Contents

For my brother, who has given me so much hope and inspiration over the years.

For my parents, who taught me more than they realized of grace.

For Val, who has been an amazing support and compassionate voice in my life.

For Christine, Nancy, Kendon, Bridgid, Mark, Andrea, and Anne, who make work a family and encourage me to grow every day.

A Solitary Daydream

I find it helps to remember in times like these
that all things are simply what they are:
whether burning fire or rain staining ground wet,
all these things are unchanged, untouched,
by even the worst chaos inside of me.

I cannot control the feelings any more
than I could halt the moon-pulled tide
or the storms of hurt that rock me,
but I can weather them with patience
and wrap myself in their ashes

I am not a phoenix blazing upward,
but I am the uncurling root and leaf
of a pine seed after a forest fire:
one part of regrowth and restoration
that sweeps across these lands.

In a world where many people
make deserts and call them "peace",
I remind myself over and over
just my love can be a droplet of water.

A Love Letter to Home

If I could trace love like a line on the page,
it would be a silhouette of the Elkhorns—
the radiant crests of the Rockies outlined in gold—
the swirling rapids turned indigo by dusk—
the eastern plains thick with buffalo grass
that extend into amber infinity,
shifting and rippling with the wind
like schools of gilded fish—
the sky transfiguring from rich azure to glimmering midnight
and back again—
the dilapidated buildings that stand as memories
of people whose dreams and hopes wore them gray and old,
weathered like the sides of their barns—

If I could hum love like a strand of a symphony,
it would be gales that rise in Big Timber,
morning and evening, like the tides of the sea—
the burble of the creeks threading the backcountry—
the roar of Yellowstone's foaming geysers and springs—
the rumble of thunder rolling over beargrass to strike at timber
stands—
the crack of rock against rock on a hiking trail,
nudged into motion by the feet of friends—

the light echoes of our voices in the Caverns—

If I could taste love like Olympian ambrosia,
it would be the honey sold off the bed of a farm truck,
just down the two lane road that turns into dirt—
pasties, onion and potato, at St. Patrick's Day in Butte—
prime Angus steak, roasted with care over open coals—
the hint of pine in the air on Mount Helena's trails—
the salt of tears shed in the arms of a friend—
cinnamon whiskey splashed into honeycrisp apple cider—

If I could feel love like the touch of your hand,
it would be the crispness of fall, when the leaves turn topaz—
the sweetness of spring rains, when the hills are still green—
the satisfaction of a shady spot beneath the blazing summer
sun—
the bitter bite of winter that aches with every breath,
because love is tumultuous and difficult as well as gentle—
the smoothness of river rocks under bare feet—
the tautness of a playing fishing line—
the rough bark of fir on split firewood against a stacking hand—

If I could let love linger in my senses like perfume,
it would be the smell of pine sap crackling in a woodstove—
the petrichor on dry buttes after a thunderous deluge—
the scent of delicate wildflowers growing blue on a hillside—
the fallen cedar needles forming western loam—
the sacred smoke of sweetgrass and sage—
horse manure and house paint and roasting fresh-caught trout—

the tang of gasoline poured into a boat's engine
before it heads down the Blackfoot River—
the smell of trail dirt, lingering like a momento
of all the atoms of our past selves,
scattered here, of all places—

The last best place, they call you.

I call you home, because love lives in your mountain lakes, your
sleepy towns, your endless beauty that reveals another fraction of
my soul in its reflection—

Every single day.

Now that You are Gone

I love you better now that you are gone.
If a wound is a place where light comes in,
My heart is drowning in the shining sun.
The days are brighter with a shattered bond.
I feel you better now that you are gone.

Tangled briars and a throne of thorns wither,
Giving way to lovely, velvet rose and vine.
The clouded cataracts of envy clear and
I see you better now that you are gone.

Lovebird sonnets from trembling lips,
A heart's desperate letters left unread,
Your voice once fell on shuttered ears;
I hear you better now that you are gone.

The ashes that have settled are my own:
The bitter curses that I once sowed,
The spurned bed that I never called home.
I love you better now that you are gone.

I cannot love you better now that you are gone.

Words come rushing, tumbling, unsaid,
As shadows of what might have been
Play like phantom echoes in hollow spaces.
I cannot hear you now that you are gone.

As elusive dancers cavort about the stage,
As vibrant colors grow from gray to glory,
Your face glows at the corner of my eye, but
I cannot see you now that you have gone.

You loved me once, but miles stretch between
That time, that place, that twisted thing.
I loved you once, as choking thorn loves trees,
As waves love the divers that they drown.

I cannot feel you now that you are gone.
I released you from that wicked spell
And now, I sleep in desolate sheets
As Morpheus spins me longing dreams....
I cannot love you better now that you are gone.

Easier

It feels easier, now that you have forgotten me.
I say this not in sorrow, not in pain, but in relief
that all the strains and sighs now leave me be.
I find peace knowing that flown is all your grief
and all the fears that kept you from being free.

It feels easier to see that the scars have faded.
I can stand open-hearted beneath a gloaming sky
and watch twilight raindrops miss earth shaded
by dark branches, without regretful sigh—
all this because the hands of Time have aided.

It feels easier to see how you move on.
Knowing that the wounds I did bleed no more,
Hearing that all the harm I worked is gone,
brings me a lighter heart, if one still sore;
your happiness shares a brighter dawn.

It feels easier to see a wish fulfilled at every plea.
On winter nights, summer days, from here to end,
may lost or absent your memories of us ever be.
It is enough to know where I cut, she may mend.

May ardent love and joy be all you ever see.

It is easier, now that you have forgotten me.

The Bitter Truth

"You are going to die."
A numbness so deep it doesn't seem real.
A delirium induced by absence, not presence.
Those words crawl into battered shoulders.
They echo through all the hollow places.
They run down a spine knotted and showing.
They trace along skin stretched tight over ribs.
They braid themselves with breaking hair.

"You are going to die."
Not a threat, but a promise if there is no change.
Not a joke, but grim certainty without pretense.
Those words slam into my anxious thoughts.
They spin a world that is already upside down.
They reflect in my funhouse mirror eyes.
They slide into my empty stomach.
They put roots into my jutting bones.

"You are going to die."
Tears bubble up like a wellspring of pain.
Tears pour down like a rainstorm of sorrow.
Those words ache in a shattered heart.
Somehow sharper than their cutting judgments.

Somehow deeper than their love expressed.
Somehow weightier than my Sisyphean stone.
Somehow harder than even a swallow.

Sixteen. Twenty-two. Twenty-seven.
Always the same, always terrifying.
Yet the course barely changes.
"You are going to die."

I know.

Agree to Disagree

"Agree to disagree," I say to myself
To a portal of polished glass,
With a twirl of skeleton bone,
With a flash of hollow eyes,
With a smile of ragged lips.
"You say you try and try, but...
I know you are no perfect thing.
You look too much, not enough.
You take up too much space."

"Agree to disagree," I say to myself,
To a window of polished glass,
With a mouthful after mouthful,
With a touch of fragile fingers,
With a glance of hopeful gleam.
"You say you try and try, but...
I become by approximations,
You look hopeful, not desolate,
You take up not what you deserve."

"Agree to disagree," I say to myself,
To a mirror of polished glass,
With a flex of muscle regrown,

With a brush of hair that bends,
With a heart that beats safely.
"You say you try and try, but...
I know you for what you are.
You look beautiful, not destroyed.
You take up just enough."

I know you will not go away,
Twisted thing inside of me,
But in the matter of thought and heart...
We can agree to disagree.

Silver Threads

I do not know if I love you.
I do not have gemstone words,
Nor love's carnation flowers.

I feel soft things in softer spaces,
I feel stirrings of regret—
Like silver threads in a spider's web.

I do not know if I love you,
I do not have a fond farewell
Nor adoration's rosy color.

I feel sharp edges in jagged splinters,
I feel absence in every touch—
Like smoke curled around fingers.

I do not know if I love you.
I do not hold the thorns of roses
Nor the quiet of falling petals.

Moths and Eggshells

The long dark night of the soul;
Is it long? No longer
than the imprisonment of a moth
within a delicate eggshell.
Unbearably long to the moth, perhaps,
but the prison cracks so easily
by accident or by intent.
And then, for the moth?
The glory of flight, delighted in, freedom!
Whether to devouring flame or radiant moon,
this is hardly the moth's concern.
And why would it be,
after surviving the intolerable?
In its wake, only cracked porcelain:
the mask, the bones, the body—
the little pieces of eggshell.

I do not love the eggshell for its strength,
nor the moth for its patience.
When one is fragility scattered,
and the other flown in relief—
perhaps I am content with the ending.

To All the Things I Have Lost

To all the things I have lost:
I scrape my breastbone for dregs of heart,
The tatters of love I give to feed you,
Until I feel the wind within my ribs,
For I held you precious above all.

To the invulnerability destroyed by illness;
To the innocence broken by breaking a heart;
To the future shattered by grim present;
To the pasts ruined by indecisive tremors;
To the strengths sacrificed by sorrows that drown;
To the skills unpolished by rusting doubt;
To the people poisoned by shuttered silence;
To the selves discarded by careless choice;
To soft things inside butchered by selfish hand...

To all the things I have lost:
I blend the blood of grief with tears of ink,
The tatters of love I give to feed you,
Until the well of dreams runs dry
From simply writing your names.

Hollow

I am from this day forward a hollow thing:
a forgotten promise, an unfeathered wing.
My words weave themselves shrouds of ink,
the chains of my thoughts rust link by link,
the dreams I chase are ephemeral breaths:
all dearest things must have their deaths.
Not now because one has gone too far away,
but because my ravens fly home to stay.

I had thought them gone to distances grayed
by all the uncertainty that Fate conveyed,
but they dust all my hours with dark feathers
and drag my heart into inclement weathers.
The bones of their wings are made of words,
their caws echo dismissals sharp as swords.
all the things I would rather not say now sing:
I am from this day forward a hollow thing.

Swallowing Stones

A lump of stone in black and blue:
The aches that settle in my chest,
The strains of being what you wished,
The torn chrysalis of future passed—
Swallowed whole is all of you.

It happens over, over, over again—
I wonder not why I cannot eat,
For I have made a meal of pain
And let self-hateful gluttony sink in—
A choking place where sorrows reign.

I would cut it out to spite my heart,
Drag shame's razor across my face,
And banish all thoughts of touch,
As its price is more than I can bear—
But that would soothe only part.

I wish I could undo my evil acts:
My selfish fears, my thoughtless snaps,
Crackling in my mind like broken glass,
But I cannot even undo yours

And all the unspoken, ugly facts.

I wish you had never laid eyes here,
For look what we have done to me!
When I open up my mouth to speak:
Nothing—Nothing—more Nothing!
Even boundless pain is unclear.

Nothing, nothing, more nothing—
That is what I wish for this.
Not salve, not soothe, not you—
Above all things, I want an end:
Nothing, nothing, more nothing.

She Loves Me Not

She loves me, she loves me not—
plucking my kindnesses
like daisy petals,
just to fling them over her shoulder.

She loves me, she loves me not—
twisting my heart
like a pinched stem,
just to drop it into the pond.

She loves me, she loves me not—
leaving me bereft in the dust
like half-upturned roots,
just to link hands with him.

Never wishing to see.
Never seeing.
Never me.

The Lilies

Give me lilies with full hands,
As if there is something left of me,
As if I did not wither on the vine.

Give me lilies with both hands,
So I may press my lips to petals,
So I may recollect myself.

Give me lilies with full hands,
With vision clearer than my own,
With voice softer than my thoughts.

Give me lilies with both hands,
And I will recall their subtle scents,
And I will hold them as my hope.

Lilies that fade in a moment...
Lilies that return every year...
To remind me of who I can be.
To remind me of letting go.

Silhouette

The brush of a fingertip across violet petals,
the rich smell of your lingering cologne...
This is how you left me:
with echoes of feathers in my hands,
fading and fragile.

The subtle sorrows that come as cobwebs fade
from glistening silver to a dull gray
are no different than the shades of clouds
I watch pass across the dome of eternal sky,
knowing you are gone.

The world is no longer what it was,
our dreams cast out as the stardust of past lives;
but scraped skin is sensitive and
a broken heart ten thousand times as clear.

So let me tell you how I see you:
how the silhouette of your back edged in silver
flashes in my dreams like sun spots from gazing
too long at Radiance itself.

You are tall, tall enough that I stand on my toes
to link my arms around your neck.
Your eyes are brown, silently sad as
I press lips to your stubbled cheek.
My fingers correct the knot of your crimson tie.
You left it wrong, so I would touch you to fix it.
When you stroke my hair, I can hear the ticking
of that favorite mechanical watch.

And when I tell you I love you, not now, but then,
It only makes the sorrow flower.
So let me tell you I love you now, not then:
Not as lovers do, but as an impressionistic
painter presses his lips to his dried canvas.
I love you for all the things you were,
all the visions we painted together,
though each has slipped from my fingers
into eternity.

A Loving Lens

To catch a kingfisher on perfect wing,
the spreading of each delicate feather,
frozen in a moment of blissful flight—
all with a simple click, a shudder of a shutter;
this would be merely the beginning,
of a love affair with light and shadow,
capturing the essence of people
as silhouette or portrait detail:
their weathering doubts and hopeful dreams
as brilliant light rediscovered in a dark room,
like Persephone descending and arising again
as a spring of life in vibrant color.

It is a delicate thing, shaken out until visible:
jubilant moments taken at the very peak of rapture
or the depths of sorrows preserved in amber,
glimpses into a past that fade far slower
than our fragile memories do,
even well-thumbed and yellow.

To tell a story in a thousand words,
never lifting a pen;
instead, to show and let my subjects speak

in silence, yet their own faces, own words.
For the very best capture things
not only as they are,
but in landscape and background and framing
more honest than a half-remembered fable.
So powerful, the very presence of them
changes our eyes' perception of the world.

Arms spread before an army—
A fist upraised in solidarity and pride—
First steps on a world so pondered at in poetry—
Starvation and a vulture—
Dust clinging to a careworn woman—
Guns and fire that mark our cruelty—
A man of purpose and a spinning wheel—
Roses and mountains tendered with love—
The powerful and the ordinary,
the expression of the human soul,
all mingled as impressions on paper,
each as unique and precious
as a grain of sand in the hourglass of Time.

Work of a Daughter

I say I love you,
when I wipe spit,
even thick with half-chewed flecks
and bitter-stinging medication,
from the chin
of the woman who changed my diapers.

I say I love you,
when I change the dressing on a sore,
oozing and angry red,
that refuses to close
on a foot
of the man who taught me to tie my shoe.

I say I love you,
when I fly across the country
just to sit and wait for 48 hours
in a hospital room,
holding a liver-spotted hand
that once helped me totter
across a toy-strewn carpet.

I say I love you,
when we walk in the house
and I catch her without knowing how,
the moment she starts to slip,
because what I feel
is so elemental to my being
that to see a bruise on her is like a stone
grinding into my own heel.

I say I love you,
when the nurse comes to take him
into the bathroom,
and I wave them away
because sometimes he cries
feeling so vulnerable
even though to him,
I am just "that nice girl"
who takes him to the bathroom.

I say I love you,
because your loves live on in me,
indelibly imprinted on my soul,
and so I will love you
without pride,
without condition,
without impatience,
without anger,
even when you have forgotten me.

And one day, I will stand
where earth is your bed
and grass is your blanket,
holding every precious moment
for as long as I can.
On that day, and every time
I think of you,
I will say,
"I love you."

For A–

In all the things that we have seen,
the raging rivers forded together,
the bitter truths that have ripped
my thoughts from what was best for you—
I know that I have not been as love intends:
patient, kind, and present.
It is a difficult truth to endure,
that such things cannot be undone.

But know, that even in the midnight hours
of the soul that stretch unbearably long
not once have I ever thought of you
with anything but the admiration
of one who wishes she was even half as strong,
nor have I thought of you as anything less
than a man of purpose I am proud to know.
While so many things better said
have gone unsaid and discarded by Time
I am so grateful for you and the time we spend,
that I taste salt as I write.

Whatever comes and goes, know this:
I carry with me the first time I really laughed in months

after you came home from where duty brought you.
I hold close knowing that even when I was sick,
you were there in the same room, at a safe distance.
I treasure the writing you have shared with me
as a trust that you have given so delicately,
jeweled and beautiful like butterfly wings.
I keep my pride in you with me like an ember
of a fire that warms when all around is cold
and I intend to tell you, at every occasion that arises,
that I was blessed beyond measure
to have you brought into my life as a brother.

For R–

I cannot think how to thank you,
except to describe the image indelibly imprinted,
by friendship that even years cannot erase,
a rare emerald in a sea of bottle-glass beads.
You do not know the full measure
of the mercies you bring into my life,
as if effortless, swept along by your coat's hem.
You are open, open as the sea is wide,
and clear in honesty as polished quartz.
Your heart you hold in your hand,
showing it with trepidation, but trust.
You take my pains and miseries
and transfigure them into molehills
instead of mountains.
I could speak to you a thousand days,
and each time feel better than the last,
for the clever working of your mind
has a way of challenging and inspiring
thoughts that might have never leapt to life.

You give your compassion so carefully,
and though you speak of fighting dragons,
I see in you the dedicated gardener,

who takes such joy in tending
people around to watch them bloom.
I do not know the measure of your doubts,
but if you could see as I have seen:
the beauty of your determined faith;
the patience with my struggling ways;
the tenderness and tough love,
applied each in their place;
the thoughtfulness, the intent
to bring shadows into light and banish them;
The confidences of shattered hearts
You let pour into your own—

I wish I could grant you my eyes,
To see yourself as I can see you:
Gardener, dragonslayer, beacon of light
even when the world is dark.
I treasure your friendship like a pearl,
taken from the deepest ocean depths
opalescent and pure
and priceless in its quality.
Thank you for the philos you have
brought flourishing into my life.
I will be here in gratitude and companionship
for however long you wish.

For P–

Since there is no mirror that reflects into the soul,
I will hold up words and show what I have found,
knowing that you might not see the flower
inside its bramble cage.

When you walk through the door frame,
your shoulders bow under the weight of the world.
The boulders of obsidian on your back,
sharp and hurtful as shards of arrowheads,
slice deeply into your peace of mind.
Your head always dips with the heaviest thoughts.

The first thing you do is ask how I have been,
and never with anything but the most genuine care:
not setting down your burden,
but shoving it to one side in concern.

Sometimes the pain and anger you carry boils forth,
in bitter words and sharpened tones, the knives of self defense,
but the moments that stay with me when you leave
are your simple acts of care.

Because of you, I have a crystal that sits beside my writing,
reflecting the light of divine inspiration,
and reminding me of unselfish compassion.
Because of you, I have a brown owl named Ozymandias,
sitting beside my keyboard and reminding me to be still and
wise.

It was once said that any
who create on earth a heaven
find the strength to within their own hell.
I believe that now,
because I have heard you speak of baby crows,
and beloved dogs held so close
their paws are imprinted on your arms in ink.

You remind me with every visit
that the most wonderful roses are found,
and shed a scent that perfumes the air around
with colors that brighten the world,
only where the thorns grow.

Memory as Echoes

Is there anything stranger than memory?
Constantly mutable, yet fixed.
Fallible, yet indelible.
The elderly woman with dementia
who hears Tchaikovsky
and again moves her arms,
a graceful swan maiden.

Some keep images tucked away
for rainy days or lonely nights.
Others, snatches of melody,
or the comfort of a familiar voice.
But as I age, I find more is memory
a part, indivisible, of you:
visible in little ways.

A tea cup stirred back and forth,
because a brother absent years
said it was more efficient.
A splash of milk
into powdered hot chocolate
because a first crush made it that way.
A crossed number seven,

because in learning numbers
a father marked his that way.
Never dogearing a page,
even on cheap paperbacks
because a librarian mother
would have pursed her lips.

My memory is not images or words,
but the echoes of people
stretching back into places,
even beyond conscious recall:
some shadowy impressions of dark emotion,
others vibrant and bold,
but every one of them lingering
like the hints of a swan's beloved song
animating a self long obscured.

Snippets (Or Three Thoughts in Treatment)

If this is what it is to be calm,
To feel the buffeting of waves
And keep the flexibility of palm,
Then let this be what saves
This endless peace of mind.
A medicine that flows, drifts...
A sheet of paper signed
And folded into white rifts,
Valleys and slopes of ink,
That memory might link.

***

Happiness is...
...a sunset edged in royal purple and golden gleam.
...a familiar song on a sun-weathered red radio.
...a roughness of old paper under fingertips.
...a perfume of clean sheets from a warm dryer.
...a lingering sweetness of mint on the tongue.

***

Quiver like a drifting feather:

Take refuge in the wind.
A bird on wing
lets go and
falls
up.

A Less than Gentle Healing

With this heart sickness I have borne,
I do not need soothing vapor or gentle word.
Its roots run so deep into my chest,
only a scalpel, sharp and painful, can reach.
I do not find relief in affirmations,
but in those piercing questions that drench the soul
in sunlight:
the only true antiseptic for secrets.
I do not find gentle footsteps healing,
for they tread gingerly around my wounds,
that same misguided timidness
allowing infection already to abscess in my bones.
I need Truth, the surgeon's knife to cut
and expose it down to its root,
before excising the cancer of the mind
that metastasizes each passing day.
I am beyond tentative measures.
No, it is purposeful and heart-wrenching
difficult things that my disease would have me
shy from, as those who treat me do,
that serve as the panacea
for the ravenous infestation in my soul.

And if it is a thing I must do alone,
and all these helpers nothing more than smoke,
let it be so
and I will draw the knife myself.

Unbecoming

When I was younger, I only heard
of growing pains and growing up,
of the careful construction of the self,
and the relentless press of becoming.
But now, as I sit at the loom of Soul
and look at the work of my inexpert hands,
I think:
perhaps I wish I had been taught
the fine art of unbecoming.

Not ending, no, but the delicate unraveling
of missed wefts and tangled fibers
woven haphazardly by unceasing hands
ever focused on the next pass.

And how to be alright
with the thought of undoing
instead of doing:
the artistry of letting go despite fear.

But how does the hermit crab
know he has outgrown his homely shell,

except by the painful pressing of the old?
So how was I to know of unbecoming
until I felt my heart restricted
by a constructed carapace,
those unkind thoughts and ambitions
cutting into a heart as it swells.

Perhaps it is not that we grow around our grief,
but that it grows around us—
not as a thing we shatter and shed,
(though one takes a cue from hermit crabs),
but as a garment needs adjustment:
one undoes the seam to let it out.

I wish I had learned sooner of unbecoming,
of the gentle easing of mistakes
by unraveling with forgiving fingers—
not to restore it to a pristine thread,
for it has stretched and worn,
but because by unbecoming,
we can practice to be a better stitch,
closer and closer approximations
to our intended pattern.

Without Space

Imagine yourself as an object without space,
no longer determined by a physical shape,
setting aside the notion of what is deserved,
and the idea of the body as a cage without escape.

Think of what the self is like when unused
lie all the measuring tapes and scales,
the mirror that torments with imperfections,
and the magazine collage of desired details.

Instead, think of the breath that animates,
slowly drawn in to expand an ivory cage,
the softest touch of breeze out across lips,
and the steady heart beating, calm as a sage.

Think of how broad and deep your loves lie,
to release the tempestuous Future and all its fears.
Think of how high and wide your hopes stretch,
and purge the sorrows past with free-falling tears.

Feel the anchoring ground beneath your feet
for it is true, even when ever-present is despair,

it requires solid footing on the blessed earth
to construct dreamscape castles in the air.

Perhaps, in such a practice, it becomes clear:
shape is better defined by what we hold dear.

Song of Myself

Strange to think, how easily others sing their song
drawn straight from their own heartstrings,
and yet I feel barely better than muteness,
Doubts crowding out the sounds of my throat.

How does one sing of their own self
when silence swallows the music
it seems everyone else can hear?

I say I could not carry a tune in a bucket
as a joke to friends, but I feel it in my pulse:
the quiet pounding until it is deafening.

So let me sing as the musician who has lost
the very hearing that taught them a tune,
but still feels the rhythm in the reverberations
that spread through the floor beneath them.

I sing myself, not as Whitman did,
and pour out all my daydreams onto the page:
those darker things that come as melancholia
and those bright flashes of connection.

I sing myself, not as a daring soloist
but as that quiet child in the back of a choir
mouths the words until they know no one is listening,
and when they are alone, let everything pour out.

How does one sing of their own self
when silence swallows the music
it seems everyone else can hear?

Not to the rooftops or public square,
but I sing defiant where it matters most:
in the echoing chambers of my heart.

Silence

The end of a poem:
silence stills the mind
as all the vibrant colors
the songbird notes of music
playing behind open eyes
drift untethered to their end.
The pause of expectation,
the hesitation of thought,
or perhaps the absence of beauty
is as potent as its presence:
a reminder that all things end
within the comfort of contemplation.

The end of a poem
stops not with the last drop
of inked hopes and dreams,
but with a soundless echoing.
It is the hollow lull
that allows all else to speak.
What is a poem without an end?
A collection of cacophonous music,
a strand of convoluted images,
confused, speaking ad nauseum.

Find joy in a silent reprieve
adding depth to your meaning.